At Heart a Romantic

Poems by

Andy Botterill

Published by Feather Books
PO Box 438
Shrewsbury SY3 0WN, UK
Tel/fax: 01743 872177

Website URL: http://www.waddysweb.freeuk.com
e-mail: john@waddysweb.freeuk.com

2006

Acknowledgement. Poems from this collection have appeared or will be appearing in the following magazines and publications: Cauldron, Dandelion Arts Magazine, Decanto, Feather Books, Linkway, Never Bury Poetry, Phoenix New Life Poetry, Poetry Cornwall, Quantum Leap and Rubies in the Darkness.

ISBN-10:   1-84175-242-8
ISBN-13: 978-1-84175-242-6

Simon Andrew Charles Botterill © 2006

No. 255 in the Feather Books Poetry Series

CONTENTS

AT HEART A ROMANTIC 4
I DON'T WANT TO GROW UP 6
MOSTLY HYDE 7
TIME IN THE SUN 8
THEY ALWAYS LEAVE ME 9
FREAK ACCIDENT 10
A DIFFERENT FANTASY 12
DEAR PARENTS 13
GOLDEN OPPORTUNITY 14
HELP 15
DECISIONS 16
TOO MUCH PLEASURE 17
ONE GOOD DAY IN SEVEN 18
IT BREAKS MY HEART 19
HIS NEEDS AND HER NEEDS 21
HAPPY 22
YOU THINK ABOUT THINGS TOO MUCH . . 23
ALONE 24

AT HEART A ROMANTIC

I could weep for the years that have passed.
I could weep for the days that are lost.
I could happily embrace every one of them,
even if at the time some were less than fun.
Now I'd happily re-live them.
For each I'd seek a new beginning,
a new way to start
and a new way to end them.

I could wear my hurt like an emblem.
Experience in all forms, for better or worse,
must surely count for something.
I could weep for the years that have gone.
Many times I have done.
I've longed to see old friends,
former lovers, past acquaintances, once again,
when I know it will never happen.
That's why I mourn.

I mourn my loss.
I carry it with me from each day to the next,
with the weight of a malignant growth.
Sometimes I'd like to cut it out,
sever all links, but I can't.
I'm hopelessly nostalgic.
I'm at heart a romantic.
I remember people as decent,
even if they weren't.
I give everything a sentimental gloss.
I prefer it like that.

I weep that our paths no longer cross.
I weep for the lost generation of my birth.
I weep not for this world,
but for whatever comes afterwards.
I weep for each and every memory I have erased,
for each and every face I can't recall,
for useful thoughts, ideas I've had
and not written down.

I weep for novels and stories
that haven't reached completion,
for risks never taken,
for countries I've never seen,
for every opportunity denied exploration,
for each flawed, poorly made decision,
for my own sense of failing.
I weep again and again.

I DON'T WANT TO GROW UP

I don't want responsibility.
I don't want to grow up.
It's not healthy.
I'm 40. I'm not 18 or 28.
I want to write poetry,
paint and record music.
I want to kick a football
round in the park.
I want days off to do what I want.
I want to catch a play
or go for a walk.
I want to stay up late watching TV
or go to a movie on a winter's afternoon.
I want to go to the pub and get drunk.
I want to hang out with my mates
until five in the morning.
I want to go to a club.
I want to chat up girls and take drugs.
I want to live in the fast lane.
I don't want to conform.
I don't want a wife and children.
I want to party until I drop.
I don't want to settle down.
Don't want a car or a pension.
I don't want a job.
I don't want to grow up.

MOSTLY HYDE

As a girlfriend she had no redeeming qualities.
She would have given him a life
of daily unhappiness, given the chance.
She was selfish, moody and difficult.
Her superficial attractiveness
disguised what she was really like underneath.
She was Jekyll and Hyde. Mostly Hyde.

He always wanted her to be something she wasn't.
He wanted her to possess feelings
like a normal human being.
For some reason
she simply didn't have them.

She was unreasonable in the extreme.
She couldn't get out of bed.
She never wanted to do anything.
She wasn't as other people are.
Now she only has herself to blame
for whatever goes wrong in her life.
She can no longer blame this person, him.

TIME IN THE SUN

We all have our time,
our moment in the sun,
days when the grass is green,
when we're fit, healthy and young.
We have our whole lives ahead of us,
lives in which we can do anything.
We think we're invincible.
Every dream is still possible.
No avenue, no path, is yet excluded to us.
We're fuelled by youthful hope.
The world is still at our feet.

We all have our time,
when we're the new kids on the block,
when we're fresh and exciting
and can carry off the latest fashion,
when our heads are full of eager anticipation.
We've not yet grown cynical
by the failure to live up to expectation.
We're not yet jaded.
We're enthusiastic and optimistic.
This feeling lasts until your early twenties.
Then slowly, bit by bit, year by year,
it gradually fades and vanishes.

THEY ALWAYS LEAVE ME

They always leave me.
That's what they do.
They always leave me,
after one year or two.
I should expect it.
I should see it coming by now.
I should have foreseen
you'd leave me too.
I should have anticipated it,
but I never do.

They always leave me,
but the reasons are usually new.
It would be easier if they weren't.
Then there would be something I could do.
They always leave me.
They tell me we're through.
They leave me and leave me
picking up the fragments and pieces,
trying to put them back together
like a complicated jigsaw,
but I never do.

FREAK ACCIDENT

A little girl was out with her mother,
enjoying a family fun day
at an army base in Germany.
Her name was Isobel Victoria.
She was the daughter of an army corporal
and she was five years old.

It was a balmy summer's day,
until suddenly without warning
the skies clouded over,
the wind gathered pace
and it started raining heavily.

The girl and her mother sought shelter
under a canvas tarpaulin,
where the little girl's arm
became entangled in a rope
holding down a large helium-filled balloon,
one of the star attractions at the annual NATO open house
summer picnic for German-based British forces.

Somehow in the high wind
the balloon escaped its mooring
and the little girl was dragged into the air.
Her mother tried to hold her,
but the wind was too strong
and she watched in shock and horror
as the little girl was carried away,
ten, twenty, then one hundred feet high
into the grey, rain-filled sky.
Her last words as she vanished were *Mummy, Mummy.*

They found her tiny body almost 30 miles away,
scattered over a wide area.
DNA testing was needed to identify her.
At the autopsy it was revealed
she'd probably lost consciousness in seconds,
before being smashed into not one
but many large buildings and obstacles on her journey.
The fact she was probably already dead
was little comfort to her grieving parents.
They wanted answers, explanations, for their loss.

At an army court martial afterwards,
several NCOs were charged with negligence
over safety arrangements at the event,
which had led to the little girl's death.
That won't bring the couple's daughter back.
They will re-live the moment
she was snatched by the wind
in their heads for the rest of their lives,
wondering how the freakish of freak accidents
could have been allowed to occur.

If only she hadn't got entangled.
If only they could have held her.
If only it hadn't rained.
If only winds hadn't reached 100 miles per hour.
If only the balloon hadn't broken free.
If only...
If only all these things hadn't allowed
this poor child, Isobel Victoria, to die.

A DIFFERENT FANTASY

He believed in care and compassion.
She saw every little human failing
as weak and pathetic.
They just weren't compatible on any level.
He wanted her to be one thing.
She wanted him to be something else.
Neither one could make the other what they wanted.
In the end they gave up.
They had to admit defeat.

For three years he created
a fantasy world in his head
which she inhabited.
He imagined she was his princess,
watching over him like a guardian angel.
She wasn't.
She wasn't watching at all.

She had a different fantasy,
one in which she was leading another life
many hundreds of miles away.
His little world wasn't enough.
She wanted more.
She wanted grander things,
something he was never quite
able to provide her with,
despite his best efforts,
despite every sacrifice.

DEAR PARENTS

Every Wednesday on my day off
I call at my parents' house for lunch.
It's no different than it was a decade earlier,
even though my mother is now 72
and my dad is 74 and in his 75th year.

It's a safe and familiar routine,
one I'd like to go on forever.
Whatever else happens
and goes wrong in my life,
I know they're there.

I sense the appetising smells of fresh, home cooking
the moment I walk through the door.
In the background is the comforting sound
of a transistor radio playing *Radio Four*.
A copy of *The Daily Telegraph*
lies partially read on a table,
the crossword started but not as yet completed.

This is how my parents live.
They're my rock, my support,
lest I should flounder,
which all too often I do,
but one day they won't be there.

I hope that day never comes.
It will be hard to bear.
I'll become the father
my daughter has to look up to.
I only hope I'm up to the task
and worthy of the example set
by my very own parents
these last trying 41 years.

GOLDEN OPPORTUNITY

We had a golden opportunity.
We blew it sadly.
I brought out the worst in you.
You brought out the worst in me.

We should have seized what
good fortune brought our way.
We should have made the most
of the love that chance blessed on us.
We didn't.

That we didn't is both
your fault and my fault,
but mostly is just a wretched waste.
Love like that is a rare commodity.
We had a golden opportunity.
We blew it sadly.

HELP

On any other day I'd have started a conversation.
On any other day I'd have picked up a phone.
On any other day I'd have asked you how you were doing.
On any other day I wouldn't have left you all alone.

On any other day I'd have asked you back to mine.
I'd have made you a coffee to help pass the time.
I'd have shown you the latest poems I've written, like this one.
I'd have welcomed your opinion and any constructive criticism.

If you'd looked a little glum, I'd have asked you how you were feeling.
I'd have asked you what you were thinking,
if you were well, if you were sleeping.
Now I have question after question.
They come into my head in the morning, afternoon and evening.
Then I had none and made my excuses and walked on.

On any other day I'd have started a conversation.
On any other day I'd have picked up a phone.
On any other day I'd have asked you how you were doing.
On any other day I wouldn't have left you all alone.

On any other day I'd have suggested a walk in the park.
On any other day I'd have told you what I thought.
On any other day I'd have paused for a moment.
On any other day I'd have spared the time to catch up.
I didn't. Now it's too late.

On any other day I'd have known that look in your eye.
I didn't and I don't know why.
On any other day I'd have known something was wrong,
I'd have spotted it at once and responded there and then.

It's alarming that I didn't. I was selfish.
I was too caught up with my own worries to notice.
On any other day you'd have asked for my help.
On any other day I'd have willingly given it.

DECISIONS

Making decisions is difficult.
Should he stay with the girl he loves,
the one he's now with,
with whom he shares a flat, a bed,
or should he look for someone else,
someone who shares his long-term outlook on life?

It's a dilemma.
Should he stay? Should he move on?
He wants to settle down, have children.
She doesn't. She isn't interested.
She doesn't want ties.
She doesn't like commitment.
The weight of responsibility
lies uncomfortably with her.

He weighs up the pros and cons.
Is there room in his life
for someone so different?
He likes days out.
She likes days in doing nothing.
He likes to make the most of his time.
To him time is valuable, a precious thing.
She likes nothing better than to fritter it away,
as if it has no value at all.

Making decisions is difficult.
At the moment he feels he's just
frittering away his life,
failing to reach a decision,
failing a make any real conclusion,
lacking the courage of his conviction,
failing to move on,
wasting his best years,
years he'll never have back again.

TOO MUCH PLEASURE

I have a confession to make.
I like a drink.
I drink more than is good for me in fact.
Before I know it,
one drink becomes ten.
I like to go out as often as I can.
I don't like to stay in.

Too much pleasure is giving
me a headache every morning.
I take everything to the extreme.
I have no appetite for compromise,
no room for moderation.
I turn pleasure into obsession,
socialising into compulsion.

The pursuit of the impossible dream
is my unsatisfied goal.
I don't stop when others would. I carry on.
I'm mildly obsessive compulsive.
It's a disorder, a disorder of the mind. Look it up.
I inherited it from my dad,
if you can inherit something like that.
It's an acquired or learnt habit,
a form of ritual that has to be carried out.

I've dedicated my life to pleasure.
I don't want to work.
I don't want to settle down.
I want sex every night,
even more if I can get it,
with as many new partners as I happen to meet.
I sense the red mist descending.
Finally, have I gone too far?
Have I had enough?

ONE GOOD DAY IN SEVEN

One good day in seven.
That's how it averaged out.
You gave me one good day in seven.
The rest of the week was best forgotten.
One good day in seven, you gave me,
sometimes not even as many as that:
one in a fortnight, the rest we don't speak about.

You gave me one good day in seven,
if I was lucky.
That's about fifty a year.
On the other three hundred days
you were as difficult as you could possibly be.
You revelled in it,
extracted delight in spreading misery.

One good day in seven,
maybe it wasn't as many as that,
Perhaps I'm being a little generous.
Memories tend to accentuate the positive,
negate the negative.
You gave me one good day in seven,
and I'm supposed to be happy with that?

IT BREAKS MY HEART

It breaks my heart to read in the paper
of the murder of innocent Iraqi children,
blown to bits by a car bomb
as they ran out into the street
to receive sweets from American troops.

It breaks my heart to read
some still had gleeful smiles
of momentary happiness
frozen on their young faces in death,
their brief joy at receiving some small gift
as short lived as their short lives.

It breaks my heart to hear
of hostage children in Africa
being forced to eat fellow captives alive
or else face murder themselves.

It breaks my heart that every second,
every minute, every hour of every day, more die,
from hunger, because we can't feed them,
from torture, from disease,
because we can't treat them,
from abuse, from war,
because we don't care.
It makes me think of my own daughter,
how it could be her,
if we didn't lead the privileged lives we do.

It breaks my heart to think
of this cruel world in which we live,
in which children have to grow up.
It breaks my heart that instead
of doing something about it,
we concern ourselves with trivia.

It breaks my heart to see
people controlled by greed.
It breaks my heart to be surrounded
by bigotry, selfishness and hatred,
one person hating another,
as if there's not enough hatred
in this world to go round.

It breaks my heart that we are
destroying our environment
and have no regard for our future.
It breaks my heart that there's nothing
it seems that can be done
to stop the madness before it's too late.
It breaks my heart to be
numbered as one of them,
to be part of this sad human race,
of the face of Capitalism and the West.

HIS NEEDS AND HER NEEDS

He's a romantic. She isn't.
That's the basic problem they have.
He dreams of candlelit meals for two,
expensive hotels and restaurants,
cosy weekends away,
long, affectionate walks,
lingering kisses,
holding hands in the park,
lying in bed making love,
watching films and TV afterwards,
sharing a bottle of wine,
enjoying quality time together
when they can.

She dreams of something different,
of meeting up with a mate,
inviting friends over,
dinner for eight,
or as many guests
as they can possibly accommodate.
She dreams of another hen weekend,
to add to those already planned,
or a girls' night out,
no partners, no boyfriends, invited.

It makes his heart sink.
Their needs aren't compatible on any level.
He's a romantic.
She doesn't believe in romance.
She won't go to the cinema
to see a film as a couple.
She has to invite someone else.
Two isn't enough, not for her.
It is for him
That's all he needs.
She needs something else altogether.

HAPPY

For the first time I'm happy for you.
I begin to see why you did
what you had to do.
You needed to be free.
You needed to be able to fly
and not be stuck here with me.
I understand that now.
I'm glad I finally see.
Before I failed miserably.
It made no sense to me.
I'm glad you're happy.
You're as happy as can be,
and I'm happy for you.
I'm glad I set you free.
I'm glad you can no longer say
your woes and ills and misfortunes
have all been caused by me.

YOU THINK ABOUT THINGS TOO MUCH

You think about things too much.
You let them go round and round in your head,
seeking answers where there are none,
and when they don't appear,
you repeat the process
and go back round again.

You think about things too much.
You always have done.
You expect honesty from people
they don't return.
You think about things too much.
You hate living in a world of lies and corruption.

You can't be one of them,
not now, not ever,
so you'll never get on.
You think about things too much,
but it's brought you only pain
without any wisdom.

ALONE

The paper on which he writes
is damp and stained with his tears.
He racks his brains,
trying to recall where it went wrong.
He puts a foolishly taken weekend away in Bristol
as the turning point in their relationship,
though he knows he's probably just fooling himself.
For her it went wrong long before that.

The worst part is the occasional
glimmers of hope.
She hasn't yet moved out.
She still has his spare key.
Until she leaves
there's still the faintest chance
perhaps it's not over.

Tragically in finishing with him,
she was, all too briefly,
the person he desperately wanted her to be,
compassionate, caring,
until in the morning
the shutters came down again
and once more he was alone.